A BIG YELLOW BOOK

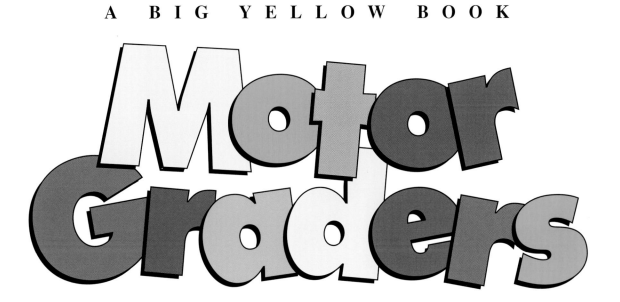

Motor Graders

Written by Jean Eick
Illustrated by Michael Sellner

VENTURE
PUBLISHING
St. Paul, MN

A BIG YELLOW BOOK

Published by Venture Publishing
315 5th Ave. NW, St. Paul, MN 55112

Designed by Michael Sellner
Edited by Jackie Taylor
Production: James Tower Media • Design
Photo Credits: "Images © 1995 PhotoDisc, Inc." Pages: 17, 20, 21
Bob Bomier – Pages: 8, 22, 23, 29, 32
All other photos courtesy of Caterpillar Image Lab

Printed in the United States of America

Library of Congress Cataloging-in-Publication Data
Eick, Jean, 1947-
    Motor graders / written by Jean Eick; illustrated by Michael Sellner.
        p.   cm. – (A big yellow book)
Summary: Gives information about this machine by listing its working parts,
describing its cab, and explaining how it is used throughout the world and
how it is constructed.
    ISBN 1-888637-05-6
    1. Graders (Earthmoving machinery) – Juvenile literature.
[1. Earthmoving machinery. 2. Machinery.] I. Sellner, Michael, ill. II. Title.
III. Series.
TA725.E37   1996
629.225—dc20   96-14127
                                                                    CIP
                                                                    AC

Contents

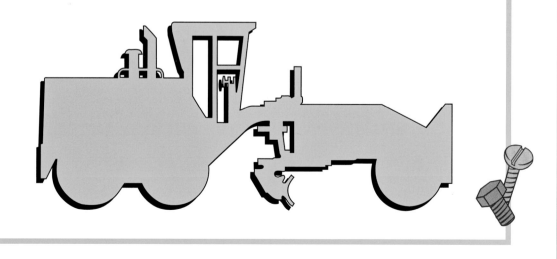

What is a Motor Grader?

If you have ever watched a new road being built, you've probably seen a motor grader in action.

The motor graders make dirt roads smooth.

A motor grader is one of the first machines used in building the road. It starts by making the bottom layer smooth and even.

As the motor grader rumbles along, it levels everything under its path.

Motor graders also help clear snow off the roads.

A long time ago, almost all roads were made of dirt. Every time it rained or snowed, the roads got very rough. Motor graders were used to make them smooth again. Back then, graders were just blades pulled by tractors.

One of the first motor graders was called a Motor Patrol.

One of the first motor graders with tires was named a Auto Patrol.

Parts of a Motor Grader

Just by changing the blades, the motor grader can do many different jobs.

Snow wing blade
A very large snow wing is used to clear snow. It can be used on either side or on both sides at the same time.

One-way blade
A one-way blade pushes snow or dirt to one side.

Reversible blade
A reversible blade moves dirt or snow to the right or left.

Moldboards (also called "blades") - The blades that push the dirt or clear the snow.

Axles - Bars that attach the wheels to the machine, and turn the wheels.

Cab - Where the operator sits to run the machine.

Engine - Where the power comes from to run the machine.

Circle - The piece that holds and moves the blade.

Wheels - Make the machine move forward or backward, like the wheels of a car.

CAT

CATERPILLAR

Inside the Cab

The cab is the little room where the operator sits. It has lots of windows, so the operator can see all around the machine. The operator uses special levers and pedals to control different parts of the motor grader. The monitor in front lets the operator know when everything is ready to go.

Everything the operator needs to control the motor grader is right inside the cab.

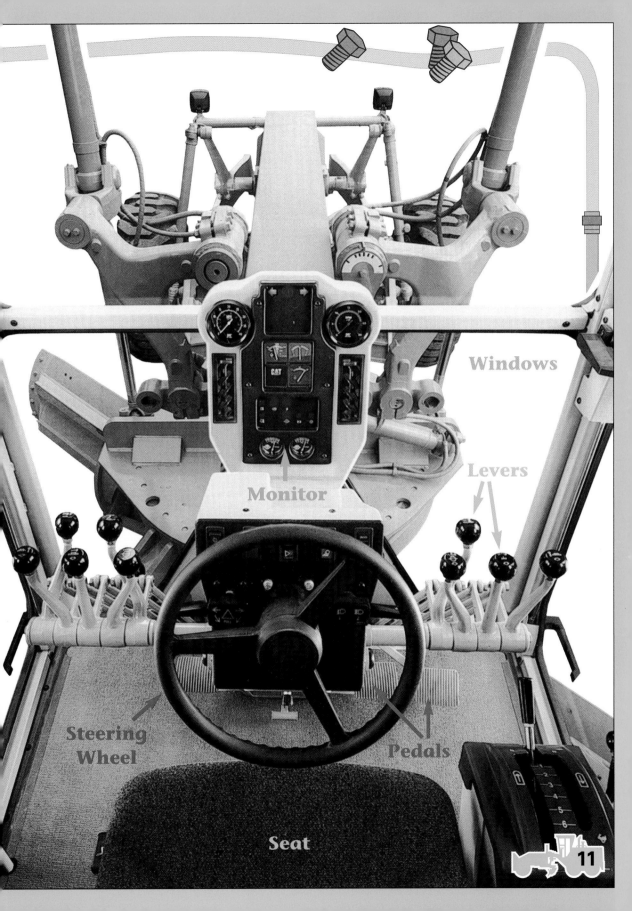

Windows

Levers

Monitor

Steering Wheel

Pedals

Seat

11

Uses for a Motor Grader

Motor graders are good machines for building roads, but they can do a lot more. When gravel and dirt roads get rough and filled with cracks, motor graders can get right to work making them smooth again.

Motor graders at work.

CATERPILLAR

Sometimes motor graders are needed to take care of the area along the sides of the road.

This motor grader cuts and clears ditches.

Winter storms don't stop people from using the roads when motor graders are put to work. That's because they do a great job clearing the snow off the roads.

Motor graders are used in open pit mines. They push coal or iron ore into piles. The piles can be scooped up by machines with shovels and hauled away in giant dump trucks.

The gigantic front shovel removes coal from the mine, while the motor grader pushes it into piles.

When the ground needs to be smooth and even, the motor grader is the machine for the job. From roads to parking lots to playing fields, the motor grader can flatten them all!

Motor graders prepared the fields for the World Cup Soccer Tournament in Chicago, Illinois.

Motor graders helped
to build these roads.

Special Facts About
Motor Graders

Motor graders come in different sizes, from large to extra large.

🔩 How Fast Do Motor Graders Go?

When a motor grader is going full speed, it can move about as fast as cars traveling on city streets. The large machine can go 25.4 miles per hour (40.9 kilometers per hour) and the extra large machine can only go 24.2 miles per hour (38.9 kilometers per hour). It's a good thing motor graders don't travel on highways. They could never keep up.

Extra Large Motor Grader

🔩 How Much Do Motor Graders Weigh?

The large motor grader weighs about as much as two large elephants (28,350 pounds/12,859 kilograms).

It takes eight large elephants to weigh as much as one extra large motor grader (122,949 pounds/55,759 kilograms).

🔩 How Much Fuel Do Motor Graders Hold?

The large motor grader holds 60 gallons (227 liters) of fuel.

The extra large motor grader holds 319 gallons (1,207 liters) of fuel. That's enough fuel to fill the tanks of about 21 cars.

🔩 How Long Are The Blades?

The large motor grader blade is 12 feet (3.66 meters) long.
The extra large blade is 24 feet (7.32 meters) long.
You would need more than four baseball bats to reach end to end of the large blade. It would take more than eight bats to match the extra large blade.

Large Motor Grader

Where in the world can you find a
Motor Grader?

People everywhere need roads to carry supplies and move from place to place. From the country roads of the Philippines and England to the city streets of the United States, motor graders are hard at work building roads all around the world.

United States

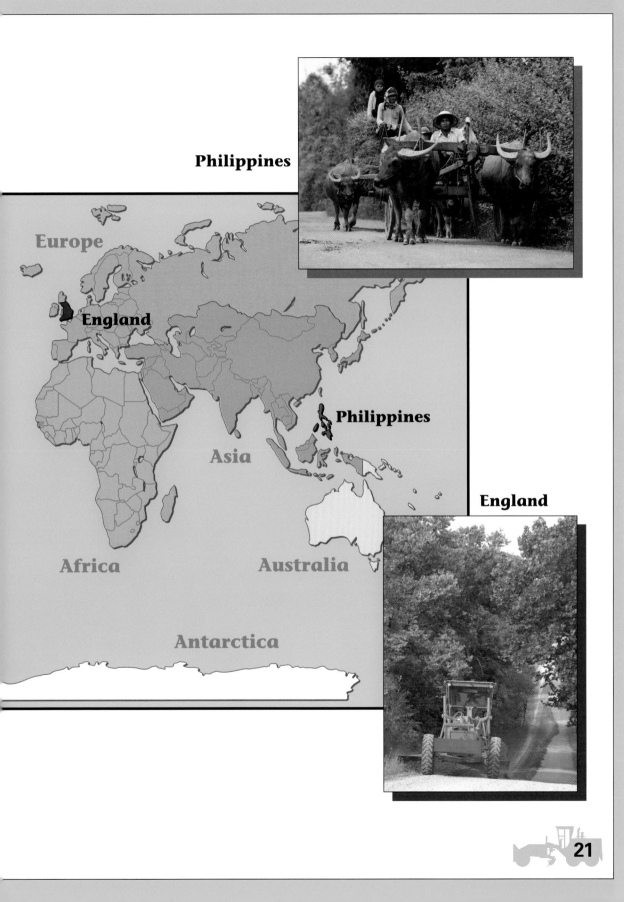

Philippines

Europe

England

Asia

Philippines

Africa

Australia

England

Antarctica

Where in the world can you find a Motor Grader?

Canada

In some parts of Canada it snows almost all year. Motor graders keep the roads clear so that people can work, play and go to school.

Where in the world can you find a

Motor Grader?

BRAZIL

Brazil is a country with busy cities and deep, dark jungles. Motor graders help build roads to every part of this beautiful land.

Some areas of Brazil do not have enough water. Motor graders help build canals, so that people will have all the water they need.

Where in the world can you find a Motor Grader? Australia

Australia has many iron and coal mines. Motor graders help move the coal and keep the roads in the mines smooth.

They also keep dirt roads open in faraway parts of Australia.

Where in the world can you find a Motor Grader?

All around the world, motor graders are at work building and taking care of roads. They help keep the roads open during the snowy winter months. The powerful motor grader is a machine that people depend on everywhere.

North America

South America

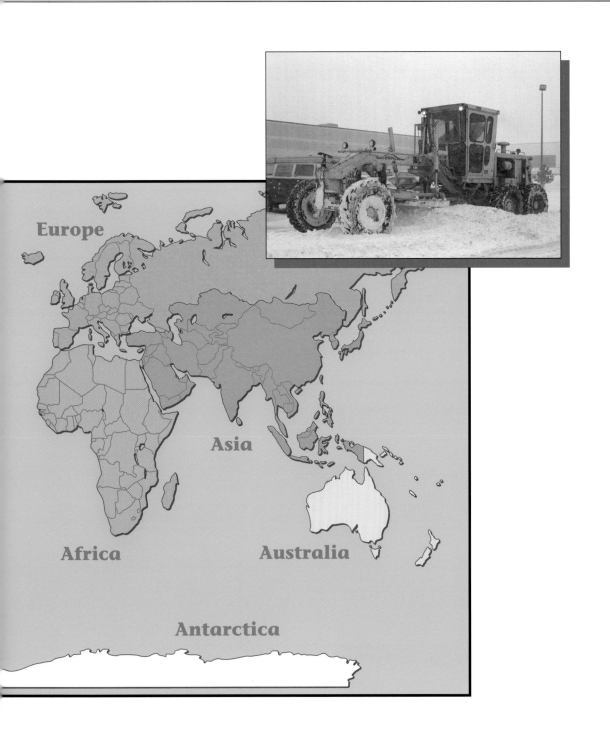

Europe

Asia

Africa

Australia

Antarctica

Putting It All Together

Before a motor grader rolls down the road, it must travel down the assembly line. Many men and women work together to build the machine. Computers help to make sure that every part of the motor grader is working just right.

Motor graders are built in huge factories.

This new motor grader
is ready for work.

Words To Remember

Circle - The round area under the front frame where the blades are attached.

Engine - Where the power comes from to run the machine.

Moldboard - Sometimes called a "blade." This is the working tool of the machine.

Motor Grader - A big machine that is used to build roads, keep roads smooth and remove snow.

Snow Wings - The large blade that is only used to push snow off roads.